CW01284678

Achaemenid Empire

A Captivating Guide to the First Persian Empire Founded by Cyrus the Great, and How This Empire of Ancient Persia Fought Against the Ancient Greeks in the Greco-Persian Wars

© **Copyright 2018**

All Rights Reserved. No part of this book may be reproduced in any form without permission in writing from the author. Reviewers may quote brief passages in reviews.

Disclaimer: No part of this publication may be reproduced or transmitted in any form or by any means, mechanical or electronic, including photocopying or recording, or by any information storage and retrieval system, or transmitted by email without permission in writing from the publisher.

While all attempts have been made to verify the information provided in this publication, neither the author nor the publisher assumes any responsibility for errors, omissions or contrary interpretations of the subject matter herein.

This book is for entertainment purposes only. The views expressed are those of the author alone, and should not be taken as expert instruction or commands. The reader is responsible for his or her own actions.

Adherence to all applicable laws and regulations, including international, federal, state and local laws governing professional licensing, business practices, advertising and all other aspects of doing business in the US, Canada, UK or any other jurisdiction is the sole responsibility of the purchaser or reader.

Neither the author nor the publisher assumes any responsibility or liability whatsoever on the behalf of the purchaser or reader of these materials. Any perceived slight of any individual or organization is purely unintentional.

Free Bonus from Captivating History (Available for a Limited time)

Hi History Lovers!

Now you have a chance to join our exclusive history list so you can get your first history ebook for free as well as discounts and a potential to get more history books for free! Simply visit the link below to join.

Captivatinghistory.com/ebook

Also, make sure to follow us on:

Twitter: @Captivhistory

Facebook: Captivating History:@captivatinghistory

Contents

INTRODUCTION 1

CHAPTER 1 – THE BEGINNINGS OF AN EMPIRE 3

CHAPTER 2 – WAR AND CONQUEST 12

CHAPTER 3 – CITIZENS OF THE EMPIRE 20

CHAPTER 4 – TRAVEL AND MOBILITY 25

CHAPTER 5 – RITUALS OF THE ACHAEMENID 31

CHAPTER 6 – FURTHER KNOWLEDGE 39

CONCLUSION 47

CHECK OUT MORE CAPTIVATING HISTORY BOOKS 49

FREE BONUS FROM CAPTIVATING HISTORY (AVAILABLE FOR A LIMITED TIME) 53

SOURCES 54

Introduction

The Achaemenid Empire is spoken about far too little. Though it was an ancient empire, their history is just as important to learn as our own.

Throughout this book, we will be learning about every aspect of this ancient civilization. First, we will discuss how the Achaemenid Empire got its start, as well as what conditions allowed their culture to grow and prosper. It will be discussed who their very first rulers were and how they decided to rule over their kingdom. We will also delve into the more prominent dynasties that occurred during the empire and how they borrowed and grew on the foundation of their predecessors.

Next, we'll be looking at the Achaemenid style of warfare. From their ongoing rivalry with ancient Greece, to their rituals used within the war, as well as what strategies and tactics they used to conquer their foes. We will also take a close look at how the empire fortified itself against intruders and the threats facing the empire.

From there we move on to a vital aspect of the Achaemenid culture, its peoples. What were their roles and obligations? Who did they worship and how? What were their beliefs?

It will be revealed how the royalty lived in lavish luxury and had their specially appointed officials carry out their wishes. From the royal courts, we move on to not only royal architecture, but also to the construction and design of all types made by the Achaemenid.

Finally, we'll take an in-depth look at the various trades routes of the Achaemenid people. The various alliances of the empire will be dissected and explained. The types of rituals that were part of their daily lives, and how those rituals were performed. We'll even get into little-known facts such as the cause that ultimately led to their downfall, the lessons learned from their history and what we can take away as a modern society.

With that said, let's delve into the fascinating history of the Achaemenid Empire.

Chapter 1 – The Beginnings of An Empire

Various records place the beginning of the Achaemenid Empire between 550-539 BCE. Cyrus the Great was credited with being the first ruler of the empire after Persians had migrated to Iran. In 553 BCE, Cyrus led a successful rebellion against the Medes (Ancient Iranians who lived in what we now call northern Iran) and founded the new civilization. Prior to the rebellion, the region was home to a number of nomadic tribes that included the Dai, Mardi, Dropici, and Sagarti. With the founding of the Achaemenid Empire, Cyrus was able to unite the various tribes and create a united Persian culture for the first time.

Stretching all the way from India to Macedonia, the land of the Achaemenids varied in climate and terrain. The Sahara Desert could be found on the southwestern border, which always maintained a dry, dusty, and temperate climate. On the eastern border, the climate was much more humid and vegetation was far more varied and plentiful. What is now modern-day Armenia was once entirely engulfed by this mighty empire. It could be that with their vast territory and as a result, significantly ranging climate, the Achaemenid Empire had the advantage over their opponents, specifically the ancient Greek population. Next, it's important to take a look at the dynasties that made up the Achaemenid Empire.

The Achaemenid Empire lasted through many dynasties. First, with the initial reign of Cyrus the Great and tracing all the way until the end of the empire, when Darius III attempted to preserve what was left of the great kingdom. Each ruler will be discussed in order of prominence and their contribution to the growth or decline of the greater Empire. We'll also examine how previous rulers were honored and how new rulers were appointed. All of those rulers would be appointed at a ceremonial capital.

The ceremonial capital of the Achaemenid Empire was Persepolis. Persepolis was located northeast of the Iranian city known as Shiraz in Fars Province. The city's name could be traced back to Greek origins, combining *Pérsēs* and *pólis* to mean "the City of the Persians" or "the Persian city." Persepolis is also situated near the small Pulvar River that flows into the Kur River. This is where Cyrus would originally settle and begin developing the foundations of the mighty and vast Achaemenid Empire.

The First Ruler of Achaemenid

It all began with one man, who would later come to be known as Cyrus the Great.

His father was Cambyses I, also known as the "King of Anshan." Cyrus would succeed his father as king instead of his uncle, Arsames. It is not known exactly why his uncle was not considered for the role, but as we look back on Achaemenid history, it's quite possible that Cambyses I saw the immense potential and drive within Cyrus that would make him a powerful ruler. By the time Cyrus came of age, he had been a war veteran and was able to directly overthrow previous Babylonian rulers. By 540 BCE, Cyrus had already begun capturing surrounding territories to add to the future Achaemenid Empire. It was only once he had conquered the whole of Babylon that he considered himself the ruler, claiming himself "king of Babylon, king of Sumer and Akkad, king of the four corners of the world."

The beginnings of the empire saw the combining of the Pasargadae, Maraphii, and Maspii tribes, which were the three major tribes of the area. Each of these tribes effectively maintained an entirely nomadic lifestyle before the empire was founded. Though it was not the first Iranian empire, that title belonged to the Median Empire. It would grow to be the largest by far. Prior to Cyrus' rebellion, the Medes were the ruling tribe, though their rule was very short-lived. This was not so for the Achaemenids, considering the term *Achaemenid* means "of the family of the Achaemenis/Achaemenes." Before Cyrus' rule, they were considered average, but with his unique leadership the Achaemenids would be renowned throughout Persia, Greece, and most of the world.

The empire itself was unified around the city of Pasargadae, which was erected by Cyrus himself. He was considered the first true king of Persia by many and even held himself as the savior of every nation he conquered.

With regards to Cyrus' character, he was a politically shrewd ruler, Cyrus made sure that everyone was free to practice their previous cultural customs within the empire. This included instating complete religious freedom, restoring temples, and reinforcing infrastructure in newly acquired cities. It's very likely that this high level of tolerance allowed Cyrus and his empire to thrive and expand over a very long period.

In the next chapter, we'll examine the methods by which the Achaemenids went about conquering and preserving their society. War rituals and battle methods will be revealed, exemplifying how the empire maintained such a vast empire, in spite of their numerous foes.

Achaemenid Rulers

Cyrus the Great, also known as Cyrus II and Cyrus the Elder, would be the first official ruler for the Achaemenid empire. He was the son of Cambyses I of Anshan, who was known as the King of Anshan. Cyrus' reign would last between 29 and 31 years.

Though his exact date of birth is still being debated, historians estimate it was between 600-599 BCE or possibly 576-575 BCE. His early life is mostly unknown, as any documents describing that period have either been damaged or lost. Over time, various folk tales emerged to describe the early life of Cyrus II, with one version citing that he was the grandson of the Median king Astyages and raised by herding folk, while another claim he was born into a poor family that worked in the Median court. Cyrus' own testimony did contradict both these viewpoints, with him assuring that he was preceded as king of Persia by his father, grandfather and great-grandfather.

Cyrus achieved his rule by rallying the Persian people in a revolt against the ruling Medes in 553 BCE. He along with Harpagus would lead his armies against the Medes until their capture of the Median ruler Ecbatana in 550 BCE.

Once Cyrus assumed his throne, he called himself the King of Persia and at that time, all of the previous vassals were effectively stripped of their previous power. Many of those vassals were actually relatives of Cyrus, who he now had complete power over. Even with those factors, his transfer of power went smoothly. He would go on to conquer Lydia, Asia Minor, Elam and finally Babylon all by 539 BCE, ultimately proclaiming himself "king of Babylon, king of Sumer and Akkad, and king of the four corners of the world.".

Cyrus would be known throughout the world for his incredible achievements in politics, military strategy and human rights and even his influence on both Eastern and Western civilizations. He would also help to clearly define modern Iran and his influence could be felt in Athens to this day.

Cyrus the Great would pass on the rule of the Achaemenids to his son Cambyses II. His daughter Atossa would marry Darius the Great and ultimately give birth to Xerxes I.

Darius the Great ruled over the Achaemenid empire at its height and was considered to be the greatest of all the Persian kings, extending the borders of the empire into India and Europe.

The government constructed during the reign of Darius would be the foundation used to form many future governments. Among his many achievements, he established a tax-collection system, a complex postal system, a network of spies called the "Eyes and Ears of the King" and built a new capital city at Persepolis. In addition, he allowed locals to keep customs and religions, built a system of roads that are still used today as well as dividing the Achaemenid empire into districts known as Satrapies.

At the height of his reign, Darius oversaw the entire Middle East, Central Asia, the Caucasus, parts of the Balkans, portions of north and northeast Africa that includes Egypt, eastern Libya, coastal Sudan, portions of greater India, the Aegean Islands and finally northern Greece/Thrace-Macedonia.

Darius established a new uniform monetary system and made Aramaic the official language of the empire. Many large-scale architectural projects were also taken under the orders of Darius, including elaborate palaces in Persepolis and Susa.

He was born the youngest of four sons in 550 BCE. His father Hystaspes was a leading authority figure in Persia. As he grew older, he would rise to the position of spearman under the rule of Cambyses II. It was even believed that Cyrus, on one of his military expeditions had a dream about Darius succeeding his throne. Cyrus feared that this could mean that Darius would ultimately overthrow Cambyses or that his son would be killed, though neither of those events took place.

Darius' rise to power had a couple different variations. His personal account stated that Cambyses II killed his own brother Bardiya, though the Iranian people were unaware of the murder. An impostor posed as the murdered brother in an attempt to usurp the throne. In 522 BCE, after growing rebellions, the Iranian people launched a revolt against Cambyses, and chose to follow the lead of the usurper named Gaumata. It was only once Darius, along with a team of other high-ranking Persians, killed Gaumata in the fortress of Sikayauvati.

Following the assassination of Gaumata, Darius and the six nobles who aided him discussed what should be done next. With suggestions of a democratic republic by one noble and an oligarchy proposed by another, Darius believed the best course of action was to push for a monarchy government. Darius stated that a republic would lead to corruption and internal fighting, while a monarchy would lead to single-mindedness and focus that would be impossible with other forms of government. Ultimately, Darius' argument convinced his fellow nobles to support him in this decision.

After participating in a strange test involving a horse's smell, excitement and the serendipitous timing of thunder and lightning, the nobles all agreed that Darius should become the new ruler of Persia. He would need to immediately quell rebellions in Elam and Babylonia after being crowned, as well as a chain reaction of further rebellions in Bactria, Persis, Media, Parthia, Assyria and Egypt. By the year 522 BCE, the majority, if not the entire Achaemenid empire was revolting against Darius. With the aid of his loyal army, which included the nobles who helped him overtake Gaumata, Darius was able to quell all the rebellions throughout the kingdom.

Though Darius had asserted his prowess through all the rebellions he had overcome, he would go on to pursue two separate and equally devastating military campaigns against the Greeks. Following the Ionian revolt and its subsequent quelling, anti-Persian sentiment and power grew rapidly with support from Athens. Darius would gather an army of 25,000 troops to march against the Greeks in Marathon. Darius' forces would be defeated in 490 BCE by a heavily armed Athenian army, with soldiers from Athens and Plataea. He would pass away before organizing a second force to invade Greece, with his son Xerxes eventually taking up the cause.

Xerxes the Great, also known as Xerxes I would be the fourth king of the Achaemenid Empire. His father was Darius I of Persia and his mother was Atossa, who was the daughter of Cyrus the Great.

Since Xerxes was not Darius' eldest son, he was not supposed to succeed him. Since he was the eldest son of Darius and Atossa, as well as a descendant of Cyrus, he was able to supersede the usual hierarchal order of succession. He was crowned in late 486 BCE at the age of 33, with a smooth succession of power.

His first achievements were ending the revolts that had broken out in Egypt and Babylon a few years prior to his rule. He appointed his brother Achaemenes to be satrap (governor) of Egypt.

Xerxes' father Darius would die in the process of preparing his plan to invade the Greek mainland, so it fell upon him to finish the job. The first part of the job Xerxes took on was bridging the Hellespont, beginning in 483 BCE, first digging a channel through the isthmus of the peninsula of Mount Athos and then building two pontoon bridges across the Hellespont.

The first attempt was unsuccessful when a storm destroyed the flax and papyrus cables of the bridges. He ordered the Hellespont whipped three hundred times and had fetters thrown into the water. His second attempt proved successful. This resulted in an alliance with Carthage, depriving Greece of powerful monarchs of Syracuse and Agrigentum. Some smaller Greek states sided with Persia including, Thessaly, Thebes and Argos.

The total size of their army rumored to be as much as two million, including a unit of 10,000 elite Persian warriors referred to as "Immortals". The true strength of the army was found to be around two to three hundred thousand and they were successful in their initial battles.

The Battle of Thermopylae was the first that was won, against King Leonidas of Sparta. Xerxes' victory drove back the Athenians and Spartans to establish their defense at the Isthmus of Corinth and in the Saronic Gulf. Apparently, some Greeks were able to spread a rumor that Xerxes had ordered Athens to be burned after it was captured, before he realized his own regret at the decision and ordered the city to be immediately rebuilt. Though completely untrue, a large portion of the Greek population believed the rumor.

Following the first battle, Xerxes made the ill-fated decision to attack a significant Greek fleet at the Battle of Salamis. The Persians were defeated, and a winter camp was set up in Thessaly under Xerxes' direction. Unfortunately, due to unrest in Babylon, Xerxes was forced to send his army back to prevent a revolt and left behind an army in Greece under Mardonius. They were defeated the following year at Plataea. The remaining Persian fleet anchored at Mycale was attacked and burned by the Greeks. That attack cut off much-needed supplies for the Persians and they were left with no choice but to retreat. This retreat roused the Greek city-states.

In the year 465 BCE, Xerxes was murdered by Artabanus, the commander of the royal bodyguard. Artabanus was the most powerful official in the Persian court at the time. There a few different accounts of how Xerxes was actually murdered and historians can't agree on one theory in particular, though it was clear that Artabanus plotted his overthrow of Xerxes for a very long period.

Though there were subsequent rulers after Xerxes, their reigns were short and unremarkable. Events would come about that ultimately led to the fall of the Achaemenid Empire and pave the way for the next empire to rise in its place.

Between 358 and 330 BCE, there were three rulers, Artaxerxes III, Artaxerxes IV and Darius III. Not much is known about these rulers, possibly due to the increasing unrest throughout the empire, during their rule. They bore witness to the final era of Achaemenid rule and the end of their civilization.

In the next chapter, we'll examine the methods by which the Achaemenids went about conquering and preserving their society. Beginning with fortifications and defenses, ranging to various war rituals and battle methods, it will be shown how the Achaemenids maintained such a vast empire, in spite of their numerous foes.

Chapter 2 – War and Conquest

The Greco-Persian Wars

It should be noted that although the Achaemenid Empire had many enemies during their reign, the most prevalent and significant were the Greeks. The rivalry between the Greeks and Persians had lasted centuries, creating a tension between the cultures that only grew over time. It would only be after the fall of the Achaemenids that the two nations would realize their similarities and be forced to learn from their differences with the rule of Alexander the Great.

The Greco-Persian wars began with an invasion in 490 BCE. Under the rule of Darius, Persia was beginning to expand into Europe and had already taking Ionia, Thrace, and Macedonia by the fifth century BCE. From that point, Darius set his sights on conquering Athens, though the reasons for that aren't entirely known. Some speculate that it was for the prestige of conquering such a prominent city while other historians claim it was in the hopes of finally eliminating troublesome rebel states on the empire's western border.

In 491 BCE, Darius sent an envoy to Greece, calling for their submission to Persian rule. In response, the Greeks promptly executed the Persian envoys, and Athens and Sparta made the promise to form a new alliance in an effort to defend Greece. Upon learning of this, Darius launched a naval force of 600 ships, containing 25,000 men that would attack the Cyclades and Euboea. This would leave the Persians a single step away from Greece.

The opposing armies would finally clash on the plain of Marathon in 490 BCE. At this time, the Persian army was around 25,000 men strong. The Greeks, on the other hand, maintained an army between 10,000 and 20,000 men, most likely nearing the lower end. This left the Greek army at a severe disadvantage in terms of sheer manpower. The Persian army employed their tactic of rapidly firing a multitude of arrows, but unfortunately for them, the Greek hoplites' bronze armor deflected the majority of them. When they met in close quarters, the Greeks were able to envelop the Persians by thinning their center and extending their flanks. It also helped that the Greek army was equipped with better armor and heavier, longer swords. They also employed the phalanx formation, a dense grouping of warriors armed with long spears and interlocking shields. This combination of factors led to a great victory for Greece, against all odds.

By the end of the battle at Marathon, 6,400 Persians had been killed while only 192 Greeks had been slain (although modern estimates are closer to between 4,500 and 5,000 for the Persians and between 1,000 and 3,000 for the Greeks). The Persian fleet was forced to flee back to Asia, though they would return again in greater numbers.

A decade later, King Xerxes maintained his predecessor Darius' vision by gathering a massive force that was set to attack Greece via the pass at Thermopylae in 480 BCE. By August of that same year, a

Greek militia led by the Spartan King Leonidas were killed after three days, except for a single man. Shortly after, the Persians entered and sacked Athens. Leonidas' brother, Kleombrotos, attempted to build a defensive wall near Corinth but was promptly halted by the arrival of winter. Unfortunately, there would be a less successful battle by the end of the year,

Toward the end of 480 BCE, there would be another battle where the Greek army would once again be outnumbered, this time at Salamis. The exact numbers are still debated, but it is estimated that 500 Persian ships attacked a fleet of only 300 Greek vessels. The Greeks had the advantage with the leadership of the Athenian general Themistocles. Having 20 years of experience and the confidence that came along with a track record of victory, Themistocles hatched a plan to entice the Persian fleet into the narrow straits of Salamis before hitting the Persian fleet with enough force that they would be completely unable to retreat. Once again, the Greeks saw victory and the remaining Persian ships were forced to flee back to Asia.

Following the Persian defeat at Salamis, Xerxes returned to his palace in Susa (one of the Achaemenid capital cities). Even after those disappointing events, much of Greece was still under Persian rule and continued to maintain a large army on land. A number of political negotiations occurred that revealed that Persia would be unable to defeat the Greek armies on land. This led to a meeting between the two armies in 479 BCE in Boeotia (a region in central Greece). At this meeting it is speculated that the Greek troops numbered around 110,000 while the Persians had a slightly larger number. Unfortunately for Xerxes and his army, the Greeks once again won the day and as a result were able to stunt the Persian ruler's ambitions.

The aftermath of the previous Persian defeats was significant. Shortly after, the Ionian states were returned to the Hellenic League who established the Delian League to ward off future Persian attacks. Though Persia remained a threat with battles continuing across the Aegean Sea over a period of 30 years, the Peace of Callias was signed by both Greece and Persia in 449 BCE. Persia would continue to thrive for the next 100 years.

Though the Achaemenid Empire could be incredibly ruthless in its pursuit for power, those who were conquered and agreed to live under their rule experienced a good deal of freedom. This included religious freedom, cultural freedom, and also the freedom to speak their mother tongue. Very few ancient cultures allowed this, making the Achaemenids progressive as a society.

Battle Strategy

The Persians were able to maintain large armies and often used brute force in their attacks. They often outnumbered their opponent but were equipped with inferior equipment. When doing battle with Greek armies, this unfortunately was one of the reasons they were defeated. However, what the Persian armies lacked in tactical precision, they certainly made up for in sheer force of will.

Generally, before a battle began, a council of war was held and plans of attack were discussed. Foot archers held the front line, flanked by cavalry which were supported by both light and heavy-armed infantry. The commander would occupy the center in order to observe and direct from an elevated and protected vantage point during the fight. From this position he was able to direct the right and left wings of the army. The first method of attack was from the arrows of the archers, before stone missiles which were intended to confuse the enemy. Lastly, the infantry moved in with their swords and spears, supported by the right and left flanks of the cavalry.

Unfortunately for the Achaemenid army, their tactics worked solely against the Asiatic armies. Both the Greek hoplites and phalanxes were able to resist the archer attacks with their body armor and massive shields. The Greeks also outmatched the Persians in hand-to-hand combat, especially considering their superior equipment and weaponry.

The great armies of the Achaemenid Empire were extremely diverse, much like the empire itself. The infantry consisted of the Immortals, the Sparabara, and the Takabara, with the eventual addition of the Cardaces (Professional heavy infantry). The Immortals, led by Hydarnes II, were considered the heavy infantry and were usually kept at exactly 10,000 troops. The name was said to have come from the fact that any sick or injured member was immediately replaced in order to maintain the precise cohesion and numbers of the group. The Sparabara, on the other hand, were always the first to engage in hand-to-hand combat in battle. Historical evidence suggests this group made up the backbone of the Persian army and would frequently form shield walls in an effort to protect their archers. The troops of this group were trained from childhood to be soldiers and would often hunt on their downtime on the plains of Persia. Lastly, the Takabara were a very rare breed who fought using their own native weapons and were recruited from territories that incorporated modern Iran.

The cavalry was also a crucial part of the Persian army and was separated into four distinct groups: chariot archers, horse cavalry, camel cavalry, and the war elephants. Both the riders and horses were generally outfitted with scale armor, wicker shields, short spears, swords, and bow and arrows. It was likely that the camel cavalry was introduced by Cyrus at the Battle of Thymbra, while the war elephants were introduced by Darius I following his conquest of the Indus Valley. This military set-up was not exactly what Cyrus the Great originally had in mind.

Cyrus had originally created the Persian military to be an entirely land-based force with no focus on naval capabilities. It was only under the reign of Darius I that the very first "imperial navy" would be created as part of the Achaemenid Empire. The navy was composed mainly of Phoenicians, Egyptians, and Greeks that would operate the combat vessels. Naval ships were originally built in Sidon by the Phoenicians and were able to transport up to 300 troops at any given time. Over time, other states within the empire began creating their own vessels to add to the Achaemenid fleet. Patrols were set up to patrol the Karun, Tigris, Nile, and the Indus. These ships were used for not only peace-keeping, but also facilitated trade.

Defense and Fortification

Persepolis served as the prime example of Achaemenid grandeur, specifically in regards to its architecture. Historians have discerned a great deal about their architecture via ancient artifacts known as the Persepolis Fortifications Tablets, dated between 509 and 494 BCE. These tablets served as a reference for the construction of the great cities of the empire, even including the wages workers were paid to build the city's structures. It also detailed many aspects of daily life of the Achaemenid population. They revealed the intricate engineering, involving weight-bearing pillars. Sophisticated Irrigation systems were also incorporated sophisticated irrigation systems within their city.

The great city of Persepolis was considered to have one of the most complex runoff and sewer systems in the entire world. The city experienced large amounts of precipitation and water runoffs from melted ice and snow during spring, which emphasized the essential need for an efficient sewer network. Two strategies were used to prevent flooding in the city. The first was to collect all runoff in a reservoir that also acted as a well, which had a square opening and was 60 meters deep. These wells were able to collect up to 554,000 liters. The next strategy was to divert runoff away from the particular structure once the reservoirs had been filled to capacity. This was done through the use of a conduit that was generally 180 meters long and 7 meters wide.

The early settlements of the Achaemenid consisted mainly of clay bricks and mud. Early Persian builders were able to create the homes as superstructures (single, undivided structures that contained no major gaps or seams). They were of simple construction, usually consisting of two to three main rooms of rectangular plan and surrounded by courtyards. Homes were light buildings with curvilinear walls and generally had fireplaces as well as furnaces. The flooring was constructed out of red ochre, which is mainly composed of iron oxide and has a deep red pigment. Methods of construction made for solid homes that could house up to nine people.

With regards to the irrigation, their system was divided into five unique zones. Two were placed on the northern end of the structure and three more were placed on the southern end. The builders managed to harmonize the system with the structures themselves by using central drainage canals in the center of the columns with small conduits and draining holes in every floor. Those holes took water out of the roof, each floor and every sewage portal and were funneled away from the structure into an underground sewage network. Each zone had a runoff capacity of 260 liters per second. This amount was far greater than what was needed, which showed the foresight of the city planners. This system handled everything from water supply to sewage management to garden irrigation within the city, which worked extremely well with the materials used to construct Achaemenid structures.

The majority of structures built in Persepolis were made largely of stone, supported with columns. Many were constructed at the base of mountains, creating additional stability. Ceilings were largely crafted from both wood and stone to reduce the overall weight. Another Achaemenid capital city, Susa, opted to use mainly mud bricks; these structures did not survive nearly as long as those built in Persepolis. Susa was adopted into the empire slightly earlier than Persepolis but was already an ancient city dating all the way back to 5500 BCE. Susa contained the palace of Darius the Great, exemplifying the pinnacle of Persian architecture at the height of the empire. It was said that Susa held such an enormous amount of wealth that Alexander the Great needed 10,000 camels and 20,000 donkeys to bring the treasures back to Greece.

Chapter 3 – Citizens of the Empire

Roles and Obligations

The citizens of the Achaemenid Empire occupied many different roles during the empire's height of power. The most prestigious of these positions was that of the Satraps, representatives of the king. Not only were they responsible for delivering his messages but were also responsible for maintaining a level of order in whichever city they were stationed. They were essentially considered governors of the state. Satrap literally translates to "protector of the province," meaning these individuals had a great responsibility bestowed to them. They would also collect taxes, control local officials, and acted as the supreme judge of the province for every criminal and civil case brought before them. Each Satrap had their own council of Persians to assist in their official affairs.

Next down the totem were the Carian soldiers and Greek mercenaries used for battle. The Carians originated from the Persian region of Caria in Asia Minor. Greek mercenaries, on the other hand, were those skilled in the art of war that were willing to fight for the highest bidder, in this case being the Achaemenid king. Both of these groups were responsible for defending the major cities, training its troops, and maintaining its military presence. Using their expertise, they were able to help strategize during wartimes and keep their armies in prime fighting condition during times of peace.

After the soldiers came the townspeople who held a variety of roles within Achaemenid society. Many shopkeepers who sold a variety of goods in the city's market square. Farmers grew and supplied food to the entire empire. Artisans and sculptors would try and sell their wares to other citizens in an effort to make a living, the most skilled of these being the blacksmiths and glassblowers. The blacksmiths were especially important, as they were ultimately responsible for crafting the arms and armor for the soldiers of the nation.

Beliefs and Worship

Throughout the Achaemenid Empire, the prominent religion of the people was Zoroastrianism. Zoroastrianism has parallels with Christianity in that there is one God who is good (Ahura Mazda) and one bad (Angra Mainyu). They considered themselves dualists, believing that light needed to be balanced with the darkness. Their sacred religious text was known as the *Avesta* which outlined the best practices for Zoroastrianism. Despite the prevalence of this religion, those that were conquered still enjoyed cultural and religious freedom within the empire. It was also essential that individuals could only pray for the good of the people, rather than just for themselves. This was one of the founding principles of Zoroastrianism.

Founded by Zarathustra (Zoroaster) who was deemed a prophet in ancient Iran, though the exact date remains unknown. Zarathustra was born somewhere around either southwest Afghanistan or northeast Iran into a culture that made use of regular animal sacrifices. His early life has little to no documentation, other than that recorded in the Gathas, which is the core of the Avesta, containing hymns said to be composed by Zarathustra himself. It is known that he worked as a priest and had three wives, three daughters, and three sons in his lifetime.

Zarathustra outright rejected the religion that the Bronze Age Iranians practiced, citing their oppressive classist structure wherein the Karvis and Karapans (princes and priests) had absolute control over all people. He was also against any form of animal sacrifice and the use of the hallucinogenic Haoma plant in spiritual rituals. Known as a sacred plant to the ancient Iranians, it was said to further healing, sexual arousal, strengthen the body, and stimulate alertness and awareness. It's unclear exactly why he was opposed to the use of the plant.

He apparently participated in a ritual using haoma at the age of 30 at the Daiti River. Zarathustra drew water from the river and when he emerged, he had a vision of Vohu Manah (Good thought). Vohu Manah took him to six other Amesha Spentas where his vision was completed. This vision transformed his worldview completely. From that point, Zarathustra was certain that there was only one true god who must be worshipped appropriately. He went about the land teaching this newfound set of beliefs to the people. Unfortunately, these ideas took a great deal of time to be accepted and his teachings were met with much resistance. Much of that resistance was most likely due to the fact that Zarathustra relegated the older Daevas (deities) to the status of evil spirits.

Zarathustra would spend 12 years attempting to spread his teachings without success before leaving his home. It was only once he reached Bactria (A historical region in central Asia) and met with the king that his fortune would improve. Upon hearing a discussion between Zarathustra and the religious leaders of the land, the king and queen adopted his ideas as the official religion of the entire kingdom. Zarathustra would pass away in his late seventies, which was an exceptionally long life for that period in history. It's possible that the values held by the Achaemenid contributed to their own long lifespan.

The values held by the Achaemenid people were few but ran deep. Aside from their god, they valued wealth and strength.

Education

With regards to education, it seems that either children were not well-educated or we haven't learned enough about the Achaemenid culture to say exactly how they were educated. From two Elamite documents, historians have gathered that young boys were taught to copy texts that were records of grain and wine being distributed. It seems that the majority of the population, including many royals, were illiterate and therefore, writing was not emphasized in Persian culture. They would generally use foreign scribes who wrote chiefly in Aramaic.

Certain Greek sources provide us with a better understanding of how Persian boys were raised. They were not allowed in the presence of their fathers until they reached the age of five, living solely with women prior to that. From that age, all the way up to the age of twenty, males were trained in archery, horsemanship, and honesty. To Persians, lying was the absolute worst offense possible, but prowess in arms was considered essential to being a man in their culture.

Royal males, on the other hand, were brought up at the royal court until they reached the age of sixteen or seventeen. There they would practice riding, spear throwing, archery, and hunting. In addition, royal boys were instructed in justice, obedience, self-restraint, and endurance.

From comparing the education of common and royal males, it's pretty evident that Persians were mainly interested in raising and training soldiers. Persian princes had even further education, learning the worship of the gods, government, temperance, and courage. It should also be noted that formal education was restricted to boys and excluded females entirely. Other than military prowess, the Achaemenid Empire did not put much of an emphasis on the education of its people.

In the next chapter, we'll take a closer look at how the Achaemenid traveled, which modes of transportation they utilized, what road systems were used, and how trade was facilitated.

Chapter 4 – Travel and Mobility

Strategic Settlements

The population of Achaemenid cities had few, but effective, methods of building their structures. For their dwellings, the houses would either be made from brick or mud. Homes would generally have one to two personal rooms in addition to a larger common area that was meant for dining and entertaining. The walls were curvilinear, often made from recovered clay blocks. Many homes were also built with fireplaces and furnaces, as well as making the floors out of red ochre. The great majority even had courtyards.

For larger buildings, there were a few options the Achaemenid builders made use of including mudbricks and also large stones. They would often either find contrasting blocks to use in these structures or painted them black and white. Superstructures were generally either official government buildings or temples. The entrances would be low and the ceilings high to increase the sense of grandeur on the interior. Tombs of the great Achaemenid leaders were often constructed in this format as well.

Routes and Transport

The routes used in the great Achaemenid Empire were absolutely critical to the success of Achaemenid Empire. The most notable of these was what they called "The Royal Road." It was a major intercontinental thoroughfare built during the rule of Darius the Great. It is actually a network of roads rather than a single one. It was designed in a way that allowed Darius to maintain control over all the cities within the Achaemenid Empire. Unfortunately, it would later serve as the very same route that Alexander the Great would use to conquer the Achaemenids over a century later.

This system of roads led from the Aegean Sea all the way to Iran, a whopping 1,550 miles, or 2,500 kilometers. The cities of Susa, Kirkuk, Nineveh, Edessa, Hattusa, and Sardis were all connected via a major branch of the Royal Road. This particular branch apparently took a total of 90 days to traverse on foot but could now be traveled a great deal faster on horseback. There were also strategically placed communication stops placed along the roads in order to maintain and speed up messages between these key Achaemenid cities.

Despite the name, this system actually included rivers, canals, and trails, as well as ports for any ships that needed passage within the empire. There was even one canal built for Darius I specifically to connect the Nile to the Red Sea. The Persians also used this network as an incredibly efficient postal system. Researchers have uncovered that the Persian Empire coveted, studied, and implemented the most essential and efficient forms of sending messages. In theory, this could be a key reason for the success of the empire. The messenger system was known as *pirradazish*, which translates to "express runner" or "fast runner."

The roads themselves were said to have been constructed from cobblestone in certain sections and made from gravel in others. Many sections were approximately five to seven meters in width, often complete with curbs made from dressed stone. Certain sections were even built with two separate lanes, pointing to an early understanding of the need for traffic control in larger societies. A total of 111 stations have been discovered along these roads, serving as both rest stops and communication points. The stations often had rectangular stone buildings containing multiple rooms. These buildings surrounded a broad market area and generally had a massive gate to allow camels carrying both parcels and humans to pass through. The largest of these way stations is reported as being an enormous five-room building, serving as a major artery for royal traffic, complete with elaborate columns and porticoes. It is believed this particular building was reserved for only wealthy travelers.

Aside from traveling on land, Persians were known to have vast fleets of military ships and a small number of commercial vessels for trade. Many citizens used horses for a faster mode of transportation throughout the empire.

Trade

As mentioned previously, the Royal Road system was crucial for both messages and parcels being delivered to and from the empire. Considering there were many Achaemenid artisans and craftsmen, the empire was definitely reliant on trade in order to grow and maintain wealth during their reign. In fact, the level to which the Persians developed trade had been previously unknown.

Considering the routes stretched from the Tigris River to Susa, served as a link between the Aegean Sea and the Transcaucasus and northern Asia, and connected the Indus Valley, it was no mystery why the empire had managed to achieve such a feat. Even the Black Sea could be accessed via the routes the Achaemenids had firmly established.

Maritime trade played a large part in the empire, with the Persian Gulf ports acting as major centers of trade with the west. Darius was even known to have a significant canal in Egypt, which connected the Red Sea to the Nile. That canal was able to provide essential access to the Mediterranean. In the beginning, this maritime trade was regulated entirely by the Phoenician merchants, but slowly merchants in the Aegean were able to gain a foothold and effectively provide market competition.

Within the empire, Babylonia was one major trade hub between Asia Minor, Phoenicia, Palestine, Egypt, and the lands of Elam and Media. Within the regions of Asia Minor, Babylonian merchants could be found purchasing wine, copper, tin, and dyestuffs. Asia Minor had both iron and silver mines to allow for such things to be sold and traded regularly. Copper, however, was mined in Cyprus, as well as the upper reaches of the Tigris, with certain parts being used as limestone quarries. Babylonians brought alum from Egypt and Syria, which was mainly used as a dye for wool. Egypt was also where ivory, gold, ebony, and certain other luxury items were brought from. Greek artisans mostly crafted the luxury items at Naucratis in the Nile Delta.

There was a famous business house located in the Babylonian city of Egibi. It played a prominent role in regards to trade, with agents buying slaves in Elam and also a number of agricultural products. Grain was exported from Babylonia, in addition to woolen clothing which was of particularly high demand, especially in Elam.

The strange aspect of all this is that overall, the exchange of commodities was very poorly developed in Persia. It makes all the trade that occurred over such a vast empire all the more impressive. The society was even known to have individuals who held the title of chief merchant.

When it came to international trade, India was a very large trading partner for the Achaemenid Empire, with their exports of gold, ivory, and aromatic oils. Siberian gold was even imported via Bactria. Greece was able to provide olive oil, wine, and especially ceramics. Greek coins became heavily integrated into the Achaemenid Empire over an extended period of time, being found from Afghanistan all the way to Egypt. Lastly, the Lydians were instrumental in their role for creating the custom and practice of retail trade.

Alliances in the Empire

The most significant of the Achaemenid alliances was the alliance formed with the nation of Sparta. Sparta had signed a treaty with the empire after the major Athenian failure during the Sicilian Expedition (An Athenian military expedition to Sicily). In addition to that, the Athenians were supporters of the Achaemenid rebel Amorges, who broke the previous agreement between the king and the Delian League. This agreement specified that neither party should attempt to interfere in the other's sphere of influence. The new alliance between the Persians and Spartans was formed in the hopes of ultimately bringing down the Athenians.

Over time, three versions of this treaty were created. The first treaty stated that everything belonging to the king shall continue to belong to the king and that Persians, Spartans, and other allies must hinder Athenians from "receiving money or any other thing." It also stated that the war against the Athenians would be carried out jointly by the king, the Spartans, and their allies. Lastly, it claimed that should a revolt occur against the king, they would immediately become the enemies of the Spartans and their allies, and if any Spartans or their allies revolted against their own government, then they would become the enemies of the King.

Historians believed this first treaty to be completely outrageous and one-sided in favor of the Achaemenid Empire. If accepted, Sparta would be forced to surrender all of Greece outside the Peloponnese. Ultimately, the Spartan government refused this version of the treaty as the terms were too unreasonable.

The second treaty imposed a rule that said "neither Spartans nor the allies of the Spartans shall make war against or otherwise injure any country or cities that belong to King Darius II or did belong to his father or to his ancestors." It went on to outline that in turn the King shall not make war nor injure any Spartans or their allies. Some of the other newer rules simply stated that the Spartans and Persians shall act jointly in all matters of war. If peace is to made with the Athenians, it must be done jointly. If a rebellion occurs within the alliance, it will be dealt with jointly. The whole idea of this newer version of the treaty was to clarify and expand on the first version. The biggest problem Sparta faced with this particular treaty was that by signing it they must refuse to found an empire. Though this treaty was agreed to by the Spartan ambassador Therimenes, the Spartans themselves were not happy about the results.

Upon a second revision, done in the late spring of 411 BCE, a third treaty was created. This third treaty was yet another attempt to clarify from the previous. Under the terms of it, Spartans would be forced to give up all Greek towns in Asia and leave them to Achaemenid rule under Darius. Unfortunately for them, they had no alternatives and were forced into a position where they would have no choice but to sign this treaty. At this time, the Athenians were still a threat and Sparta needed the help of Persia to have any chance of defeating them. As such, the king was in a position to demand absolutely anything of the Spartans. The strange thing is after that trouble in finally achieving a somewhat successful treaty agreement; both sides ended up ignoring the terms, though the reasons are still unclear exactly why this occurred.

Chapter 5 – Rituals of the Achaemenid

Ritual Importance

Achaemenid culture involved many rituals involving all aspects of life. This could be due largely to their belief that their deity required these rituals be adhered to in order to bless the people. It could also have simply been a function of finding that ritual behavior made for a healthier and more productive society. Whatever the case, we will now take an in-depth look at exactly what rituals were used in their culture and why.

The vast majority, if not all of the Achaemenid rituals, were based on their religion of Zoroastrianism. Many of these involved an animal sacrifice as a sort of tribute to their god, but they also held a great reverence for fire. They knew that fire held great power, both for destruction and creation. The people even considered fire as a symbol for truth. Horses were often sacrificed, some in hopes of either cleansing or strengthening the soul, while others attempted a sort of divination, known as hippomancy, in an attempt to make use of a horse's behavior.

The culture did still incorporate sacrificial rituals along with many other rituals. There was a ritual for burials and one for the dead, to honor their memories and to help their souls transfer smoothly into the afterlife. Communal feasting was another mainstay in the community, believing it to bring about bountiful crops and, consequentially, full stomachs. Lastly, household rituals were performed regularly in an effort to cleanse homes and ward off any negative energy from entering or staying in their respective dwellings.

Some rituals were exclusive to the nobility. When it came to the king, it was considered in very poor taste to meet his gaze directly, and as such, elaborate rituals were enacted where courtiers and visitors to the royal palace would receive extremely limited access to any royal personages. It is said that even the king's footstool was loaded with ritual, even having a court of the office associated with it. This was backed by the idea that the king's feet should never be forced to make contact with the bare ground and must be protected with soft carpets, though this was not the only formal ritual.

There were also formal greeting rituals. One in particular was said to have been performed by the chiliarch and it was a gesture of obeisance to the monarch; this greeting was in fact used in later Muslim courts. One such ritual involved the dead.

In addition to sacrificial rituals, there were also rituals involving the dead. One was a burial ritual derived from the Zoroastrian religion. It was believed that bodies should not be buried because they were unclean and that the demon Nasu immediately rushed into a person's body moments after their death, not only contaminating and putrefying their insides, but also everything around them. In fact, it was preferable to leave the bodies for wild animals to consume. Even still, certain parts of the population did not adhere to this rule and found ways of burying their loved ones. The worst penalty for being caught performing a burial was what amounted to a moderate fine. It was also widely believed at the time that the land where an individual was buried would only become pure again after a period of fifty years.

Some of their lesser described rituals involve glass production and certain cult rituals. These were likely performed in an effort to create good fortune in their lives and honor their god at the same time. It is quite evident that the Achaemenid people appreciated and valued the importance of rituals in everyday life, so much so that it became a major part of their culture.

Festivals

In the Zoroastrian religion, the people of the Achaemenid held two different types of festivals. The first involved the seven feasts of obligation, otherwise known as Nowruz, as well as the six gāhānbārs. Together, these made up the framework of their religious year and it was even considered a sin not to adhere to these traditions. The other category was divided into major and minor feasts. The major feasts were kept throughout the community, in honor of the *Yazatas,* which were a class of benign divinities of Zoroastrianism. There was one exception to this, which was Frawardīgān and Sada, a winter and fire festival. Not much was recorded regarding the minor feasts, many of which were held in honor of the *Yazatas*.

Annual festivals were held at pilgrim shines during appointed times. Some of these festivals evolved spontaneously; one such festival was the Sasanian feast of Ābrīzagān, which was essentially a Persian version of Thanksgiving. Smaller, occasional festivals were celebrated at various times throughout the year, usually by families or a local community. These smaller events were referred to as *yasna*, which is just a generic Zoroastrian term for a festival.

All Achaemenid festivals included one or more acts of worship. These services could be anything from the long and elaborate *Visperad*, celebrated at every one of the seven obligatory feasts, to the *yasna*. A simple Āfrīnagān sufficed for more minor occasions. Every *yasna* was a holy occasion, and those who participated were supposed to be in a state of physical and ritual cleanliness. They believed that dirt and pollution belonged to the evil spirit and would prevent any prayers and worship from reaching divine beings.

The obligatory festivals on the other hand, would only permit necessary work, likely referring to any duties required to set up and maintain the various festivities. During the first part of these festivals, participants would wear their very best clothes and enter houses that had just been scrupulously swept and cleaned before being part of religious services and saying their own respective prayers. If for any reason they were unable to adhere to that process, they would take part by sharing the food offered and receive a blessing. During the festivities, merriness and joyfulness was encouraged, as this was seen as a weapon against sorrow and care. It was considered Zoroastrian doctrine joyfulness and was considered to be a virtue. As with all Zoroastrian festivals, food and drink made up a prominent part of the events.

Traditional festal foods were assigned to specific festivals and wine was regularly consumed alongside the food that was served. There was almost always music played at each event, and dancing was commonplace. Many of the musicians were women who were permanently attached to the sanctuary where the festival was being held. Story-telling, play-acting and miming were also incorporated into various festivals, with some even holding chariot-racing events. Others used different athletic competitions as alternative forms of entertainment.

Economy

As a direct result of the pre-existing developed economies within the Achaemenid Empire, the socioeconomic structure of the empire was characterized by extreme diversity. This included the regions of Syria, Egypt, Phoenicia, Babylonia, Asia Minor, and Elam and included the Sakai, Lycians, Nubians, and other tribes that were in the process of leaving their primitive social structures behind. Due to these factors, the economy of the empire remained largely decentralized throughout its reign.

Through agriculture, the Achaemenid economy was stimulated over a long period of time. Even the cities were largely agricultural, with the urban population being fully engaged. Their most bountiful crop was barley, which was grown in Babylonia, Egypt, Elam, and Persia, with wheat and spelt being lesser crops.

Three basic economic sectors existed within the empire. There was the royal sector that was managed by the king's chancellery, the sector that was owned and operated by the religious temples, and the private sector. Under this system, all agrarian lands were measured and divided, with the very best being distributed to the king, business house, the temples, military elite, and civil servants of the royalty and temple administration. Certain portions of the king's land were leased out to the royal managers. The Achaemenid kings even owned forests in Syria and the right to income from fish caught in Lake Moeris in Egypt.

Large estates of conquered peoples were said to have been distributed between members of the royal family and Persian nobility. They would hire soldiers to till their plots of land and settled those of various ethnic origin on state lands. During this time, the soldiers were required to pay royal taxes and serve their respective conscriptions.

The royal sector also owned large workshops throughout the Achaemenid Empire, where goods would be made in mass quantities and distributed throughout key cities within the empire. According to Greek historians, around 15,000 people were fed each and every day at the cost of 400 talents of silver. Officials would be placed in the employ of vast royal properties and were tasked with the management of the royal sector. The entire sector was comprised of more than 100 towns and settlements in Persia and Elam and divided into six different districts. It was served by more than 16,000 workmen, ranging from stonemasons and master woodworkers to shepherds and beer brewers.

The economic sector that was managed by the temples was the most abundant for Babylonia and, to a slightly lesser degree, Egypt. Both large estates and handicraft centers were owned by temples in Babylonia, while landowners were forced to lease out part of their land-holdings as a result of insufficient staff of agricultural workers. It also seems that meat was actually part of the daily diet of Persians even though most other countries would consider it to be a luxury.

The primary source of state income for the Achaemenid Empire was taxes, with a considerable portion set aside in royal treasuries. These taxes were required to be delivered in the form of unminted silver and were evaluated by both purity and size. Those individuals living on the borders of the Achaemenid Empire not only paid taxes regularly, but often delivered gifts. The Persians, however, were completely exempt from taxation and forced labor as they were considered the ruling people, though they were only truly exempt from monetary taxes and not all taxes.

Within Persia, coins were not used in circulation even though Darius I introduced the gold *daric*, which formed the basis for the Achaemenid monetary system. Coins were mainly used in Asia Minor and when exchanging for goods with Greece. Workers were generally paid in unminted silver goods and products. This included the highest officials and those employed in the royal sector.

Achaemenid Diet

The Achaemenid people had a great affinity for food and the customs in which they ate. The British Museum states, "Ancient Persian cuisine was highly developed, with specialty cooks, armies of servants and elaborate dining etiquette. Seating plans were complicated and banquets were typically composed of several different courses." They made use of gold and silver vessels for the majority of their meals which made by highly-skilled craftsmen who sometimes came from as far as India or Egypt. The state even provided workers' meals as partial payments in addition to their salaries. As many as 15,000 men would dine three times daily at the court of the Achaemenid emperor. What's interesting is that, even with the opulence of the Achaemenid feasts, each dinner was organized economically and not at all wasteful. This occurred even more so under the reign of Cyrus with people eating only what was needed for work and exercise.

Those who attended these royal feasts were first required to "bathe themselves and then serve in white clothes, and spend nearly half the day on preparations for dinner," according to Athenaeus (A Greek rhetorician and grammarian). This was a clear example of how highly cleanliness was regarded when dining at the royal court. The main item of cutlery that was used was actually the knife, which was to be held in the right hand. The left hand would hold a piece of bread before the food was cut with the knife which was then placed on the bread. Only after this should it be placed in the mouth.

The main ingredients used in ancient Persian cuisine were often fruits, nuts, and saffron. There were even cooks who specialized in dairy dishes. According to the Macedonian writer, Polyaenus, the king's dinner would consist of "sweet grape jelly, candied turnips and radishes prepared with salt, candied capers with salt, from which delicious stuffings are made, terebinth (from pistachio nuts) oil, Ethiopian cumin and Median saffron." Dates, figs, pomegranates, apples, almonds, raisins, and quince were common fruits used in Persian cuisine and staples of the Achaemenid diet.

The Achaemenid diet was incredibly varied, making use of many livestock animals including sheep, goats, lamb, cattle, horses, gazelles, geese, goslings, pigeons, small wild birds, and chicken. They also incorporated certain nuts and oils, as well as sweet apple juice and conserve of sour pomegranates. There was also the use of three different grades of wheat and barley flour, corn, and rye.

The king's kitchen sourced its cooks from around the world, allowing the most skillful to use their artistry to create new and exciting dishes while still maintaining more traditional fare. With this progressive thinking, the Achaemenid Empire was able to elevate its cuisine to an internationally renowned level by importing recipes from around the world and making use of the varied and plentiful talents of their chefs. They also began to export their foods, mostly to Babylon.

Some very interesting developments have occurred within recent years with dishes previously linked to certain countries actually being proven to have come from the Achaemenid region. For example, the first pizza ever made was apparently a flatbread, topped with cheese, dates, and herbs, cooked on a metal shield which effectively served as a stovetop pan. Another example would be the discovery that pasta had actually been developed in Iran first and not China. Finally, there is some speculation that Persians were the first to incorporate sugar into their dishes and possibly even the first to think of boiling drinking water in order to rid it of harmful bacteria before consumption.

Another interesting fact is that ancient Persian kings would take the time to tend to their gardens personally. These gardens would often have fruit trees, as well as health-giving and healing herbs.

Unfortunately, over time the Persians began to ignore the very dietary habits and foods that had originally kept them vital and healthy, eventually succumbing to opulence and over-indulgence. It was said that these factors greatly contributed to the Achaemenid downfall by the time that Alexander the Great moved to conquer the region. Prior to their downfall, Persians were an austere and straightforward people, with discipline and an appreciation for everything they were fortunate enough to have.

Chapter 6 – Further Knowledge

Lesser Known Facts

The Achaemenid Empire was actually considered to be the world's first true "superpower." It maintained dominion over 44% of the world's population at the height of its power, which has not been surpassed to this day.

Even rulers who were conquered by the Achaemenids experienced a certain level of freedom under the empire. Many Persian rulers even sought council from those former kings in an effort to gain a better understanding of how to rule its own peoples. This was considered an incredibly progressive attitude at the time and showed how forward-thinking the Achaemenid Empire actually was. A charter was even made, known as the Cyrus Cylinder. It was made in an effort to uphold the rights of common Persians and is considered to be the oldest known charter or symbol of universal human rights. Its premises included tolerance for each and every race, religion and language which was supervised by the ruling class, allowance for slaves and deported people to return to their given homelands, and the complete restoration of destroyed temples and religious buildings in their commitment to maintaining religious freedom within the empire.

Achaemenid armies were arguably said to be the very first to maintain a uniformed appearance through near-identical regimental dresses. This was quite unique in ancient times, especially considering how the Greeks much preferred to take a decentralized approach with their armies and were inspired by their individual *poleis* (City-states in ancient Greece). Persia was clearly much more centralized with their military, often sending out groups of 50 or so men led by the son of a noble. The ancient Greek historian Herodotus even claims that men were liable to be conscripted into war until the age of 50. Their national army, at its height, was said to be 120,000 men strong.

Apparently, the ancient Persians had a certain obsession with the number 1,000. This led them to create regiments of a thousand soldiers each, known as a *hazarabam*. They would often combine ten of these regiments to form what they called a *baivarabam* of 10,000 men. The chosen of these were known as the Immortals, or *Amrtaka*, and were chosen exclusively by the king himself. They would often flaunt their vibrant, ritzy uniforms and armaments. The insistence to maintaining 10,000 men in this group was so pervasive that the moment a soldier was sick, injured, or killed, he would be immediately replaced in order to preserve their precise numbers.

The Achaemenid empire is credited with the development of organized cavalry forces; in the latter half of the fifth century BCE, they used shock cavalry that mirrored the knightly class of Medieval Europe. The cavalry was often used as an armored battering ram that would smash through the enemy in their column-like formations. Some of the elite cavalrymen would even participate in joust-like duels, pitting commanders or kings of opposing forces against each other.

Historians have also uncovered that in later years Xerxes began to create a more mercenary-based military with much more multicultural influence. Ethiopian marines were said to have helped during the Battle of Salamis and possibly the Battle of Platea. Xerxes even incorporated certain military strategies from India and Asia

Minor in an effort to diversify its military prowess. Ironically, throughout the reign of the Achaemenid Empire, their largest source of mercenaries were the Greeks. Greece's geographical aspect actually played a crucial role in establishing the realm as a major pool of mercenaries. A few reasons for this were their pastoral tendencies which allowed women and older folk to maintain the lands and animals, while men were free to take part in military activities that occurred outside their borders. Some of the high-ranking mercenaries were even given tax exemptions and situated in strategic settlements, in order to mitigate the threat of unrest.

Ancient Persia, though often portrayed as incredibly lavish and opulent, was not always so. It was only once rebellions began springing up in nearly every corner of the empire, as well as a number of defeats at the hands of the Greeks, that Xerxes, in disgrace, began retreating into the luxury of his court and harem. This particular trend would continue for over 150 years, leading to the rise of power of the satraps. Eventually, the Persian Empire degenerated into a weave of decentralized, autonomous zones. With the arrival of a Macedonian prince named Alexander, wielding exceptional military prowess and leadership skills, he would launch an incredible invasion from across Europe.

Purple, it seems, was a very highly coveted color in ancient times, with the Persians' favorite being "sea-purple." The dye for this particular purple could only be found from a bromine-containing reddish-purple byproduct from the murex shell. This color and dye were so widely coveted that even imitations of the color were far out of reach for any common citizens to afford. Many Persian royals would often hoard the value and status associated with clothing of this color and subsequently given as gifts to higher ranked officials. What's even more interesting is that Alexander the Great found an enormous stash of the purple-dyed clothes in the royal treasury at Susa. Amazingly, these garments still maintained their rich color even after 190 years of storage.

The Fall of the Empire

Shortly after the death of Xerxes in 465 BCE, Persia was left without a strong leader. All of his successors were ill-equipped to rule over the Achaemenid people, and as a result, the problems present within the empire only grew. With the increasing decentralization and chaos, provincial satraps stepped in to assert their power and attempted to increase it by battling other provinces. The more this occurred, the less united Persia became, making it extremely vulnerable to attack. Satraps even created their own foreign policies while they waged war on each other.

Throughout this period, the government took a heavy-handed approach by hoarding its own gold and silver while increasing taxes for the population. Naturally, this led to revolts within the empire which spurred the government to further increase taxes and continue hoarding wealth. Throughout this chaos, satraps were gaining more and more power and independence from the state. It was only with the rebellion of the prince, Cyrus the Younger, against his brother, Artaxerxes II, that things reached a tipping point for the Achaemenid Empire. When Cyrus was defeated, the army of 10,000 Greek mercenaries that he brought with him was stranded in the heart of Persia without a leader. To return home, they were forced to march and fight their way through a large portion of the Persian Empire. This event was later referred to as the March of the Ten Thousand and was a perfect example of the glaring weaknesses of the empire at the time.

It was only after these events that Alexander the Great was able to invade and conquer Persia with a relatively small army in a remarkably short time. The Persians did survive and managed to reestablish their empire to create the Sassanid Empire in 224 CE, though that empire fell in 651 CE to the Arabs, who were inspired by their new religion of Islam. Nevertheless, the Persians were able to pass their culture on to the Arabs, thus the Islamic culture that emerged was ultimately Mesopotamian in origin. Finally, in 1501, the final Persian Empire rose under the Safavid dynasty and their cultures and traditions still live on today in what we know as modern Iran.

Modern Takeaways

The Achaemenid Empire had a long and varied reign over most of what we refer to as the Middle East, Asia Minor, and even parts of southeastern Europe. Throughout that reign, Persia had some incredibly progressive views on society, but also some incredibly limiting ones. From taking a close look at their successes and failures and relating them to our modern-day society, we can gather insights on how best to function and maintain our good standing in the world.

Let's start with their stance on religious freedom. Though the majority of citizens living within the Persian empire were Zoroastrians, all those that were conquered were granted permission to continue practicing their original faith and customs. This was incredibly progressive for the time and we can learn a lot from this today. What would the world be like if all people were allowed to freely express their faith, without fear of judgment or persecution? What if different religions could co-exist in the same society without violence or the threat of war? Though this does occur in some parts of the world, it most certainly could be improved and also spread to many more parts of the world.

Simply because two religions emphasize and uphold different values does not mean they are contradictory. No religion should be held as better or worse than the other. There isn't a single individual who is righteous enough to even make those claims. All religions can be used as both a moral compass and a set of guidelines to follow in one's daily life. One can even exempt certain things that do not apply to their particular situation or environment. Religion would then be used as a foundation for which an individual can act from in order to achieve the greatest good possible.

Next, let us look at how they treated food in relation to their lifestyle. Though they did hold communal feasts for holidays and celebrations, they understood that it should not be taken for granted. They also understood that a varied diet was tantamount to a healthy lifestyle. Their approach to eating only what they needed to fuel them for work or exercise can be used as an approach to modern life as well. If one only eats what is needed to sustain them for daily essential activities, that would completely eliminate the need for excess. That could include fast food, binge-eating, excess drinking, the use of hard drugs, and many more unhealthy behaviors. We would even see a massive reduction in the obesity rate in the Western world as a result of this approach. As a side effect, many people would even have the opportunity to save much of their money as a result of spending less on extraneous expenses.

If people ate this way, it's plausible that many farmers would actually see their quality of life increase drastically. With more demand for fresh and healthy food, fields would be better maintained and there would be a greater effort to grow a variety of crops in order to satisfy the consumers. It's even possible that many fast food chains would go out of business as a result of this new, healthier economy. We could even see a drastic increase in the average person's lifespan and longevity.

One could even examine the final period of the Achaemenid Empire to see what happens when opulence and extravagance become the primary values of a society. Once Xerxes had failed to maintain a successful reign and experienced a number of defeats at the hand of the Greeks, his next step was to retreat to the riches of his kingdom and his palace. Sadly, this would become the prevailing trend for subsequent rulers of Persia following Xerxes' death.

What we saw from this was a series of power struggles, greed, and decentralization of the entire empire. It seems that seeing their ruler retreat created a ripple effect throughout the empire, with some seeing it as an opportunity to further their power and influence with others simply accepting defeat without any hope of redemption. One could say that we see examples of this today.

Take for example, the United States. If we look at the never-ending clash between liberals and conservatives, we have a prime example of this type of power struggle. Both sides claim that the other is entirely false without acknowledgment of any validity to their argument. This same division trickles down to the general population of the United States. With both sides seeing each other as enemies, not only can they not find common ground, but in extreme cases they don't even acknowledge the other side as human beings at all. This is an incredibly dangerous viewpoint to have which can lead to bigotry, nationalism, and even killing.

Lastly, we can follow their example of using rituals of all sorts to improve our daily lives within modern society. There has been a plethora of studies regarding how rituals affect people and how great an impact incorporating them into one's daily life can actually have. Time after time, these studies have proven that rituals are critical in maintaining order in an individual's or even a group's life. The Achaemenid people must have realized this as they performed their own rituals on a regular basis. From the communal feasts, they would've learned the importance of community as well as food and nutrition. Surely those who participated in these feasts felt a much closer bond with their neighbors and a greater sense of well-being by taking the time to get to know their fellow citizens and break bread with them. That communal aspect would have only been strengthened during an individual's prayers, knowing they must pray for the good of all, not only for themselves. This must have constantly reminded them of just how important the people that were living in the same nation really were.

In the case of their burial rituals, their view did have some merit. Considering they saw dead bodies as unclean, they likely avoided any contamination from those bodies that could have transmitted to a living person. It also surely prevented the contamination of such things as farmland or key waterways that would inevitably poison a great majority of the citizens of the empire. Though it may have been for more spiritual reasons, it was still incredibly effective in preventing disease from spreading.

Conclusion

The Achaemenid Empire stretched over a great many countries, over a considerably long era. They did, in fact, achieve the distinction of being the very first superpower and quite possibly one of the largest in history to this day. They were able to develop and maintain elaborate and complex societal structures to maintain their rule and allowed their people to flourish. During their pinnacle, ancient Persia was nearly untouchable by any opponents or outside threats. They were, in simpler terms, an extremely well-built empire.

Even with all of their incredible achievements and solid infrastructure, they were not without flaws, and those flaws would eventually be the downfall of the empire. One of those flaws was forgetting why the empire was founded in the first place.

The original idea behind the founding of the empire was simplicity and a monotheistic view on spirituality and religion. For many dynasties, this approach worked perfectly and Persia reaped the benefits. But over time, human error reared its ugly head. Later rulers would succumb to the temptation of excessive greed and ignore the needs of the empire, its people, and Persia at large. Xerxes would be the first, but not the last ruler to experience the dark side of power and retreat to his royal chambers, surrounded by his riches and disconnecting from living beings. Naturally, this would lead to decentralization and the rise of independent sects of power through power-hungry satraps, fighting to increase the influence of their own territory.

Those satraps would use any means necessary to defeat the other provinces of Persia, often resorting to extreme measures. The direst of these being the contracting of entire armies of Greek mercenaries who are only loyal to whoever has the ability to pay them the highest wage. Of course, armies wouldn't last long and those that were successful would eventually succumb to corruption or greed and often rebel against the very people that hired them.

By the time Alexander, the prince of Macedonia, learned of the state of Persia, all he needed was a small army to conquer the large empire and claim his rule of the kingdom. Though subsequent empires did rise from the ashes of Achaemenid, none reached close to the power and reach of that first glorious empire created by Cyrus.

The Achaemenid Empire may have fallen, but it should be never forgotten.

Check out more Captivating History books

THE GRECO-PERSIAN WARS

A CAPTIVATING GUIDE TO THE CONFLICTS BETWEEN THE ACHAEMENID EMPIRE AND THE GREEK CITY-STATES, INCLUDING THE BATTLE OF MARATHON, THERMOPYLAE, SALAMIS, PLATAEA AND MORE

CAPTIVATING HISTORY

BABYLON

A CAPTIVATING GUIDE TO THE KINGDOM IN ANCIENT MESOPOTAMIA, STARTING FROM THE AKKADIAN EMPIRE TO THE BATTLE OF OPIS AGAINST PERSIA, INCLUDING BABYLONIAN MYTHOLOGY AND THE LEGACY OF BABYLONIA

CAPTIVATING HISTORY

SUMERIANS

A CAPTIVATING GUIDE TO ANCIENT SUMERIAN HISTORY, SUMERIAN MYTHOLOGY AND THE MESOPOTAMIAN EMPIRE OF THE SUMER CIVILIZATION

CAPTIVATING HISTORY

Free Bonus from Captivating History (Available for a Limited time)

Hi History Lovers!

Now you have a chance to join our exclusive history list so you can get your first history ebook for free as well as discounts and a potential to get more history books for free! Simply visit the link below to join.

Captivatinghistory.com/ebook

Also, make sure to follow us on:

Twitter: @Captivhistory

Facebook: Captivating History:@captivatinghistory

Sources

1) https://web-b-ebscohost-com.ezproxy.humber.ca/ehost/pdfviewer/pdfviewer?vid=2&sid=73abadeb-a048-4a51-b963-5da5208bf741%40sessionmgr103

2) https://search-credoreference-com.ezproxy.humber.ca/content/entry/wileyempire/achaemenid_empire/0

3) https://web-a-ebscohost-com.ezproxy.humber.ca/ehost/ebookviewer/ebook/ZTAwMHhuYV9fMzEyMjAwX19BTg2?sid=6af0a853-a885-4339-9e06-12de84f5c4b7@sessionmgr4006&vid=0&format=EB&rid=1

4) https://web-b-ebscohost-com.ezproxy.humber.ca/ehost/pdfviewer/pdfviewer?vid=1&sid=cc13d925-afb3-4ab4-aca7-6696d2203417%40sessionmgr102

5) https://web-a-ebscohost-com.ezproxy.humber.ca/ehost/pdfviewer/pdfviewer?vid=1&sid=9fc067aa-fbee-43c0-9f13-10851fba05f6%40sessionmgr4007

6) http://muse.jhu.edu.ezproxy.humber.ca/article/316364

7) http://www.achemenet.com/fr/

8) https://ebookcentral-proquest-com.ezproxy.humber.ca/lib/humber/reader.action?docID=912165&query=#

9) https://www.ancient.eu/timeline/Achaemenid_Empire/

10) https://www.ancient.eu/Persian_Wars/

11) http://www.iranchamber.com/history/achaemenids/achaemenid_army.php

12) https://www.thoughtco.com/royal-road-of-the-achaemenids-172590

13) http://www.iranicaonline.org/articles/commerce-ii

14) http://www.livius.org/sources/content/thucydides/the-treaties-between-persia-and-sparta/

15) https://persianthings.wordpress.com/2013/02/07/the-royal-court-in-achaemenid-persia-a-few-thoughts/

16) http://www.iranicaonline.org/articles/burial-ii

17) http://zoroastrianheritage.blogspot.com/2011/07/achaemenian-persian-kings-table.html

18) https://www.realmofhistory.com/2015/09/26/10-facts-achaemenid-persian-empire-army/

19) http://www.flowofhistory.com/units/pre/2/FC15

Printed in Dunstable, United Kingdom